HEALING

THE PROCESS

FATEMA KAPADIA

In the world full of broken people be someone comfort.

In the world of untrustworthy people be someone trustworthy.

In the world full of nepotism be someone saviour.

In the world full of error be a programmer.

In world of hate be the love.

In the world of ego be the gentle.

In the world of race be someone to Hold in hard.

Treat this world as you want to be treated .

Some times you and your soul know the suffering then anyone else do .

Contents

Contents

Foreword

We all are injured some and how

People we love the most has broken as the most by anything.

But at the end we all end up with scars and tears but are we truly healing? Or just pretending for healing .

The best part of pain is you know how it hurts so you must also see if you don't hurt other by same thing.

Come joint with me in the journey of injured to healing.

Acknowledgements

My mother always tell me

"Belving in one self is necessary"

As a child i use to fail is every dam subject my teachers in school always tell me i had no future but dreams are the one how make you alive .

Today also some people say "You have wasted your degree of computer if you cant find job in IT."

well i really thank them all for making me belive in my self by saying me all this things .

"Thank you "

The journey of life is not always easy some days are good and some bad .

Like that my life is also a rollar costar some time it goes high and some it goes low

This dream of being author would not be possible without Notion press .

I really bow down to my publishers and also my readers to always belive in me .

This would not be possible without them .

My first book "The rape viticm - the fight from world" had given me strength to write for humanity and also spread awarness about it .

I personally thank my parent and my husband to always support me and belive in me .

1. Lesson 1

People come and go .

It's like you know 100 peoples

But from that 100 people only 50 knows you and from that 50 only 10 cares about you.

So stop caring for 100 just care for 10 .

<u>Note :- if you try to care only about your people life would be more easier</u>.

2. Lesson 2

The process of healing is not at all easy so stop saying to you and other to move on as it take ages to forget.

Sometimes you don't miss peoples but the memories that hits you hard ...

<u>Note :- You destroy yourself for others but you get more of you after healing</u>.

3. Lesson 3

• 3 •

Nothing can be get without sacrificing.

Success needs time ,

Love needs sacrifices ,

And life needs one of this .

<u>Note :- When you sacrifice your most important and most loveable things then and you go for your goal.</u>

4. Lesson 4

You can't be good in everyone's story every time.
Even trees shades its leaf in spring.
<u>Note :- Be yourself first people see you according to there</u>
<u>needs .</u>

5. Lesson 5

When people around you change
When your trust on people looses
When every door close towards you .
When your heart is getting heavier.
When your eyes can't hold the weight of water .
Then remember god is seeing something you have not .
Then remember he is emptying place which is not of them .
Then just take a breath , look and walk .

6. Lesson 6

<u>Don't stop being good.</u>

When you do good it automatically comes back to you .

No matters if the opposite person has bad intentions or might be use you for your goodness.

But remember if you do good to others god will protect you and they will be good on the way.

7. Lesson 7

<u>***Never leave the side of truth.***</u>

No matter how had the way of truth is .

No matters how strong the false is .

No matter how many people will be against you .

But what matter is that how you face them all .

8. Lesson 8

When quietness hurts you ,
when slience becomes your sound ,
when action become you emeny ,
And you relase its your own war ,
At that time people change too .
Note :- When you are fighting for your own you always need a
soft heart to understand.
So now you can also be a soft heart for others too..?
There was a fine quote that i read on Intagram.
"Every soul is fighting there own fight.
Every quietness can't be ego."

9. Lesson 9

"When you find your efforts are worthless to others then stop being nice."

Note :- you know when to stop being nice ?
When the other person don't even care for your emotions and your sacrifice .

10. Lesson 10

Living in reality .

Living in reality is harder then anything.

Reality hurts you ,

It kills you with the presence.

But remember to face the reality for being strong.

Note :- when life becomes unfavourable and you want to skip it then remember running will make you week but facing the reality will make you strong.

11. Lesson 11

Don't stop your way as you are alone.

Remember people always leave in week part .

Note:- The society always treats strong people good though they are incorrect, though they are wrong , though destroyed everything from the power of money.

So stop trusting society only trust your part and what you are doing is right trust me .

12. Lesson 12

I know money can buy everything.

But the good heart and peaceful soul can win anything.

Note :- people offend fall for money but is this right ?

Money can be the biggest star but when the darkness appears the star get hidden.

But good and peaceful soul is the cloud which is there even when the star shines and even when not.

13. Lesson 13

• 13 •

When people remove you from their hearts they don't care about penny of suffering you are doing so stop hurting yourself just to show them how hurt you are.

Note :- As a human you should be firstly polite to your self every ending is the starting of new chapter.

14. Lesson 14

"Anger :- just unsolved sadness in peoples heart."
But what about the damage it give?
Sometime anger don't give damage it can give relief too.
Sometimes it smooth's your heart .

Note :- people offend see anger but it is also important to understand why too.

15. Lesson 15

<u>**Running is not the solution to any problem but facing them can fix it .**</u>

Lets deal this with example.

Let's take a pot what if the pot gets hole and water start to leak.

Now what you will do ?

Will put the pot on another place ?

Or will you empty the water ?

Putting the pot on another place will not stop the water but it will wet other place too .

But if you empty the water , find out the hole and then fix it maybe that will stop water to wet other place too .

So like this don't run from problem infact try to solve them think about the problem then try to find why ? Then try to find How ?

When you get answer of why the answer of how will be half across.

16. Lesson 16

"*Like circle don't have end , problem also named after circle which have no end .*"

Note :- problems are like mountains when you see from far you see as even but when you see from near you see the uneven rock also ..

17. Lesson 17

"*Is the land , power , money is important then a innocent lives .*"

Note :- when power increases people on earth find themselves above from other people and results into disrespect , indifference and egoism . But just take a moment to see that all people have blood in veins which is red in color of every human every single human take oxygen and throughout carbanion oxide . Is there anyone who've other colour of blood running in there vines or they breath carbanion oxide and throughout oxygen.

Why to difference in human if we all have same blood and same process.

Think it ! I know your heart will be agree on my words.

18. Lesson 18

"<u>We all are afraid of being left out.</u>"

Note:- From childhood we all have taught of if you will not run fast you will be left all alone .

But now growing up I realized that being alone is not harmful or shameful but you can save your self from being destroyed.

19. Lesson 19

"Sometimes messing up is ok!"

Note :- you not need to have right decision all the time.
Like trees don't have the leaf's permanent like that your decision can't be permanent till last breath.
People change, decision change, time changes everything.

20. Lesson 20

"In life it's not important how many thing you achieved but how many deeds you did to make you human by spreading love and humanity."

Note :- Doing things for the sake of giving has always loved by god.
There is a lesson I learnt from Quran saying when you kill a person it means you kill the whole mankind but if you save a human life it means you have saved mankind. The way of kindnesses must be the most most difficult but the truth is the hardest part is the part of god.

21. Lesson 21

"In the world full of situationship choose someone or be someone to choose your love and friendship all the time without hesitation."

Note :- Leave a person who choose you according to there priorities.

Because love and friendship both are priority less things .

All there is permanent meant to be things.

If they leave you when there are with someone who they thinks better then you and ignores all you worth to them then save your heart from being damage.

You always do is wait for them and they don't even look at you .

Some goodbyes are most difficult and unimaginable but the truth is you have to , if you want your heart to get pain free and your mind stress free.

22. Lesson 22

Note :- Finding trustworthy relationships again in this generation is not a easy task .

When you come across the heartbreak moment you realize the person who was the most important to you is the person to whom you are not that important

When that relationship ends without a word then you loose the hope to find that type of vibe again in your life maybe you find different but you can't replace that relationship to any of it .

Let's say if your only bestfriend from more then 5 years ditch you for that 2 year friendship you get dishearten that's how the life work the person you are confident of not leaving but they had leaved you for some other and that Is so hard to digest.

But the only thing you have to remember that people change if you are the same as you ever 5 years back then it's ok you are not that two face person you are the person of heart and you deserve much better but don't trust some one so easy to fill that empty place fast to get relief from that emptiness but that will cost you more damage so take your time and find the right vibe .

• 23 •

23. Lesson 23

Is it important to kill oneself then to stay ?
Well as an person we all think to end our life but we always forget about the person how will be left with pain after us.
Is ending up is so easy then holding it for our loved one's ?
Holding up may become hard but process is also important .
May be fixing is not easy but trying is also important .
May be threapy is not acceptable but accepting is necessary .
May be saying about mental health is shameful is scoiety but yes it is important .
Note :- Why mental health is so much shameful in our scoiety like phisical healthy it should be also common .
Like people get cold and cough but eating cold or any thing like that people also get depress by the end of some relationship or losses in life .

24. Lesson 24

"<u>There is a thin line to understand about being Alone ad being lonely.</u>

<u>Alone is your choice and lonely is being left out.</u>"

Note:- As a human I took a long time to understand this difference.

Being alone is your choice it is you your priority.

But being lonely is about your expecting the things .

In this let's take a example .

Assume your self in party or some social gathering there you enjoy being ' Alone' as you have priorities your self and explore your self you feel confident about it.

Now let's assume you are with a group of people and they doesn't carry about you and your priorities.

Now there you feel 'lonely'.

25. Lesson 25

May be that was oki to cry.
May be the hole is still not filled.
May be the eyes still need strength to see this .
As it's not easy to move on.
As it's not easy to take all the broken pieces and joint it again.
As it's not easy to believe in oneself again on the matter of trust.
As it's not easy to learn about love and hope again.
But darling dont hold the things too triedly ,
you plam is getting all the scares like your heart ,
free your plam you free your heart .
Its life maybe or likely to happen .

Note :- Leaving may not be easy but holding is making more difficulties for your to breath.

26. Lesson 26

We always forget to see loose while seeing profit is the balance sheet of life

Note :- As an human we always see profit of oneself and thats normal we all do it

but sometimes we also need to see the loose which took place while gaining profit .

while calculating balance sheet we realize we came far of loose to gain the unwanted profites .

27. Lesson 27

" Let your wing be open

Let you voice be clam

Let your hand be stronger to hold yourself

Let you be you

Dont let this world to treat you less then anything."

Note :- After certain age we realize that Maturity is not just to grow up or live alone but to relaize where relationship cant be premanet all the time .

Some fight , some moves to be taken alone , some decision , some slot of time is just you and your journey .

28. Lesson 28

Expecting for other is oki but have you ever think of expecting from yourself too.

"How i can impose my self on someone

How i can heal on depeing on others

How i can deal when i need someone "

The reason people cant heal is because they depend on other rather then there own self.

when people get hurt they run to other people to say that they got hurt by them but the forget that they are human too they can also get you hurt.

remember when you are in depression and trying to heal or want to come out of loose then flow this step

1) Stay away from people how bitch on the back of others may they are always saying to other about you.

2) Read good books, work on your self, try to speand more time with you { as in the end it is you only for you }

3) Dont trust people easy as they have stamoch which you dont know about.

4) Free your self give space and try to know about your self

.

5) Live on time.

6) Dont be the part of a big group stay up small and try to do the things that stops your overthings.

7) If you self the emptiness then deep clean your house .
8) Try to see your childhood photos {avoid if it flash back your depression }
9)Stay up true .
10) Lastly be your self again.

29. Lesson 29

Standing on little bitter turth ,
falling in the memorise of january ,
realizing how far i had came to find me ,
Scrolling my phones memory ,
realizing how can a year change the bond .
People go far , people came near ,
life turned out unimageable .
Telling oneself again and again ,
December had came ,
Now please let go ,
Now please dont hold your memory ,
Now please big your heart ,
Now please dont step out in this fack world with real heart.
Now that you are young enough to let go ,
please now welcome your self first then others .
No its not selfishness its your self prioriting your self.
Make a note to this january ,
"I am enough to my own ".
-Note to december

30. Lesson 30

<u>*"This too shall pass "*</u>

Rember nothing is Permanent every thing has to pass .
Dont froce your self for being prefect all the time .
you are not late nor you are early , you are prefect on our time.
Some get married early because it was there time,
some got married late because it was there time ,
some got job immedately after graducation,
some have stuggled for years and years .
some got there love without any problem .
some have scarifice there love for someone.
There is a small saying
"Never fight with bad time as it will not stay forever ,
Never wish more happiness for good time as it will also not stay forever".

31. Lesson 31

"The blue and red pen was for me ,
The struggle was for me ,
The hardship was for me,
The broken pieces are of me ,
Now that joining is necessary for me to accpect by others ,
Now the jounery is much difficult for me to do that,
some people got the thing easy , some with hard ,
some got sorrow , some got happier .
Living was necessary , then loosing oneself.
For me working is necessary , then spending ."

Note :- people telling enjoy your life this age will not come , go on trips ,

but we are people with no money so we dont fellow this lines.

we are the people who have lost hope in everything ,

we are the people who have lost in the battle of love ,

some destiny are written with golden or sliver pens ,

but some are written with blue and red pens too.

But what is important how you understand your own thing ,

People can go because then can .

Isnt fair if we destory are 2bkh for bungalows ?.

Think !

32. Lesson 32

"<u>Process of Healing requires Time .</u>"

Sharing your pain again and again will never let you forget

,

Try not to share your pain your weakness to many people ,

Because in this world broken people are the most weakest people,

Try to share with the most trustworthy person who can help you to get heal , not with the person how always ask about why? and how ? .

Sharing may fell you good but whom to share and where to share is your path of choose .

No one will help you in the process of healing at some point your person will leave you with any reason at the end it is you with you.

so trust your self first then others .

33. Lesson 33

"Insult :- An Untold emotion of weakness "
This word hold more distruction then any other word.
People how insult others for showing up there powers and fun for minites or two they dont know the feeling which that person holdes the whole day or even for life every single word is repated in there minds every time .
"Is being polite to someone will make you weak or make your power small ?"
No it wont but it will increase your power and respect .

34. Lesson 34

"The closest people can betray you,
broken hearts can be healed with love,
ease comes with hardship,
Being sad doesnt equal to being ungrateful,
And people with patience have beautiful endings."

Chapter35

"some get is eailer , some get it late.
some get it easy, some with hard .
Some get gold , some wait for dimond.
No one is wrong ,every one is at there place .
NO high , No low .
You are what you was supposed to be ,
So My Love "you are not late",

36. NORMALIZATION

• 36 •

Most important part of healing is getting things "Normally" we people has Unnormalized so many things. Seeing others we have froced ourself for being like them but froceing creates more prombles then being oneself , when you try to froce something either it breakes or it damage to other .

When you understand that heart breaks , faliures are the part of life then you try to normalize things as they are .

Normalization is part of accepting the process .

In the world full of Envy try to accept the process when you stop doing like others you will realize how simple is art of living .

We are the people who makes our life difficult by seeing others

In the world full of <u>Star bucks</u> high rated coffee

"Lets just nomalize "Adar wali chai ""

In the world full of "smart watches "

"Lets just normalize "Analogue watches""

In the world of series

“Lets just normalize movie like "Kuch Kuch hota hai "”

<u>*In the world full of "fancy and rich wedding"*</u>

<u>*"Lets just normalize the "simple and classy wedding*
""</u>

In world of "war"

“Lets just spread "peace" ”

In the world of being "selfish"

"Lets spread "humanity""

In world full of race to success

"Lets just normalize spending time with you and your loved ones "

Let It Go

"Let it go if its not yours,
Let it go if it hurts you,
Let it go if you cant hold any more,
Let it go if it want to ."

Listen me now ,

The person who wants to go will go at any cost , infact when its cost of your life too .

Let them finish there role , Let them go ,

Freeing someone is important to heal your self,

The more you will hold the more hate will create in you and in other too .

Remember when a person decided anything they will do it .

Like that when you decided to move on you will start .

Take little little step every day and one fine day you will joint all your parts.

I know the scratches will be there , but now find some to love you with all the scares and scratches.

Remember the process is not easy dont froce yourself to do anything as i say "Be polite to yourself first ".

Handel your self with care and love . If we cant love ourself then how we can love others ?

After every hardship there will be easy and peaceful life too.

And here i take a leave , i hope my word will give you light and hope in your life .

Who so ever reading this book remember i am with you .

You people can connect me on gmail at fatemakapadia105253@gmail.com